Chief Seattle

By Kira Freed

Wright Group

The McGraw·Hill Companies

Photograph and Illustration Credits

©AP/Wide World Photos, pp. **28** *bottom*, **29**; British Columbia Archives H-02498, p. **14** *bottom*; ©Comstock/Getty Images, p. **4** *bottom left*; Courtesy of the Burke Museum of Natural History and Culture, Catalog number 1-11421, p. **22**; John Fleck, p. **7** bottom; ©The Granger Collection, New York, pp. **4** *bottom right*, **5** *top left*, **9**, **11** *top right*, **13**, **15** *bottom*, **16**, **18** *top*; ©Historical Society of Seattle & King County dba Museum of History & Industry/Corbis, p. **19**; ©Hulton Archive, Getty Images, **cover** *bottom*, *back*; Courtesy Library of Congress, p. **5** *bottom right*; Museum of History & Industry, Seattle, pp. **5** *top right*, **10** *left, right, bottom*, **11** *top left, bottom left*, **18** *bottom*, **26**, **28** *top* vintage color postcard based on an 1864 photograph by E.M. Samis; ©John McAnulty/Corbis, p. **20** *top*, **30**; ©North Wind Picture Archives, pp. **5** *bottom left*, **8**, **11** *center*, **12** *bottom*, **17** *top*; ©Rubberball Productions, p. **11** *bottom right*; University of Washington Libraries, Special Collections, **cover** *top*, **title page**, pp. **12** *top* NA1515, **4** *center*, **7** *top* NA4025, **15** *top* NA4026, **17** *bottom* (detail) NA1522, **20** *bottom* UW 25093z, p. **21** A. Curtis 5895, p. **25** NA1536 p. **27** *top* NA1426, *bottom* NA1425; ©Ron Watts, Corbis, p. **23**; ©Mike Zens/ Corbis, **14** *top*.

www.WrightGroup.com

Wright Group

Send all inquiries to:
Wright Group/McGraw-Hill
P.O. Box 812960
Chicago, IL 60681

ISBN 1-4045-3354-0
ISBN 1-4045-3422-9 (6-pack)

1 2 3 4 5 6 7 8 9 BSF 11 10 09 08 07 06 05

CONTENTS

HISTORICAL TIME LINE

This book is about Chief Seattle, who lived from 1786 to 1866. During his lifetime, U.S. expansion disrupted forever the traditional ways of his people, the Native Americans of Washington's Puget Sound region. The rest of the world was changing during that time, too. Did you know that photography was invented in 1839? Or that surgical anesthesia was invented in 1842? This time line lists the important events in Chief Seattle's life, as well as other events, discoveries, and inventions in the world during his time.

George Washington becomes the first president of the United States.

Hudson's Bay Company builds a trading post along the Columbia River in Washington.

Chief Seattle is born in the Puget Sound area of Washington.

1786   1789   1832   1839
1787   1808   1836   1847

Chief Seattle becomes an important leader of Native groups in the Puget Sound region.

The United States Constitution is written.

On March 6, the Battle of the Alamo takes place in Texas.

Louis Daguerre invents the process of photography.

A law is passed limiting the workday in U.S. factories to ten hours for women and working-age children.

Elisha Graves Otis invents the first elevator.

Puget Sound settlers name their settlement after Chief Seattle.

Isaac Stevens, the newly appointed governor of Washington Territory and Superintendent of Indian Affairs, arrives in the Puget Sound area.

The Yakima War begins.

On November 11, Washington becomes a state.

Chief Seattle gives his famous speech during treaty negotiations with Governor Stevens at Point Elliott.

Chief Seattle dies at age 81 on the Port Madison Indian Reservation.

1852   1861   1866   1889

1848   1854   1865   1887

The California Gold Rush begins.

The American Civil War begins.

The American Civil War ends.

On April 14, President Lincoln is assassinated.

Dr. Henry A. Smith's version of Chief Seattle's speech is printed in the *Seattle Sunday Star*.

AUTHOR'S NOTE

Chief Seattle was a significant leader among Pacific Northwest Native groups for more than 50 years. During the 1800s, white settlers came to the area and changed traditional life forever. Like the history of other Native Americans after Europeans arrived, the story of Chief Seattle's people is a sad one. Native cultures across North America were forced by the United States government to give up their land and traditional way of life. The government had better weapons and a mistaken belief that they had the right to take the land for their own.

Over time, Chief Seattle became a leader dedicated to peace. He hoped his people and the settlers could live together in harmony and learn from each other. It's hard to know whether his actions were guided by a true belief in peace or whether he simply made the best choices he could to protect his people from extinction.

Some of Chief Seattle's story will remain a mystery forever because of incomplete written records. Still, from reading about his life, we can learn about a difficult time in North American history and how one man led his people through it. As you read, see if you find inspiration in Chief Seattle's story.

Kira Freed

CHAPTER ONE

A LEADER EMERGES

Around 1806, tribal leaders in the Puget Sound area of Washington learned that more than one hundred warriors from enemy tribes were gathering to attack. Earlier raids by enemy tribes had caused the deaths of many people and the capture of others to be kept as slaves.

Tribal elders understood the seriousness of the situation and considered many defense **strategies**, but they could not agree on a plan. When they opened the discussion to everyone, a tall, young member of the Suquamish tribe named Seattle spoke up. Although inexperienced as a leader, he suggested a plan

The Puget Sound area was home to many Native American tribes including Chief Seattle's.

so clever that the leaders accepted it immediately.

Enemies came to Puget Sound by canoe.

Seattle learned that the enemy tribes planned to approach by canoe down the White River at night. He led his men to a bend in the river where the currents were rough. They chopped down a large tree, stripped its branches, and positioned it crosswise a few inches above the water's surface just downstream from the bend. Armed with bows and arrows, the men hid in the brush nearby to await the canoes.

When the first raiders came downstream, their canoes hit the tree and **capsized**. Many men drowned when they were thrown into the rough rapids. Other men made it to shore but were killed by Seattle and his band. Other raiders still upstream from the ambush pulled their canoes to shore and fled on foot.

DID YOU KNOW... Before the arrival of white settlers, Seattle's people had no metal tools. Cutting down a tree was a difficult and time-consuming process. Men set a controlled fire to burn through the base of the tree. They used bone wedges to control the direction the tree would fall.

Chief Seattle's ideas allowed Native Americans and settlers to live together peacefully.

Seattle's brilliant strategy earned him the respect of his people, who paid **tribute** to him in a celebration lasting many days. His military skills led to other victories against enemy tribes as well. Because of his courage, leadership abilities, and gift for public speaking, he became an important leader of six tribes, including the Suquamish and Duwamish.

For many years, he fiercely defended his people from their enemies. Over time, as white settlers arrived in the area, Seattle became a peace leader instead of a war leader. He dedicated the rest of his life to living in harmony with white settlers while working to protect his people's land and culture.

LEAP BACK IN TIME

Life in Chief Seattle's time was very different from life in modern America. Before white settlers came to the Puget Sound region, his people, the Coast Salish, had no metal tools. They also had no written language. Their lives were centered on their canoes and the rich resources provided by the water near their homes. Fishing, hunting, digging for clams, and collecting wild plants were among the most important activities. The resources provided food, clothing, shelter, tools, medicines, and items for ceremonial use and play. Below are some of the things Chief Seattle's people used in their daily life.

TOGGLING SPEAR POINT

MAT HOUSE

NEEDLE

CANOE
BAILER

HORN
LADLE

FISHING
IN CANOES

BARK
SHREDDER

∾ 11

CHAPTER TWO

EARLY LIFE

hief Seattle was born around 1786. His father was a Suquamish chief, and his mother was the daughter of a Duwamish chief.

When Seattle was born, the Puget Sound area belonged to a group of Native American tribes called the Coast Salish and had not yet been visited by white settlers. Seattle's people and neighboring tribes survived by fishing for salmon, digging for clams, and hunting deer and elk. They gathered roots and berries to eat and also used plants to make baskets, clothing, and medicines. The plentiful resources of the ocean, bays, rivers, and forests allowed Seattle's people to live comfortably and enjoy a rich cultural life.

Native Americans spearing fish

In 1792, when Seattle was six years old, the British ship H.M.S. *Discovery*, captained by George Vancouver, arrived in Puget Sound. Captain Vancouver's job was to survey and map the coastline so that other ships could safely navigate Puget Sound and Great Britain could take ownership of the area.

George Vancouver, English navigator

Because they had never seen Europeans before, Seattle's people were **wary** at first and kept their distance. They lost their fear when they saw that the visitors were friendly, offering guns, blankets, and metal tools in exchange for local meat, fish, and furs. Seattle began to believe that peaceful cooperation was possible between the different groups of people.

DID YOU KNOW... Chief Seattle's birth name is not known. He was called Seattle by white settlers, who were not able to pronounce his original name. His name is sometimes written as Seeathl, Seathl, or Sealth.

Modern Native Americans preserve tradition at an inter-tribal powwow.

During this time, many different tribes lived in the Pacific Northwest, each with its own language, art, and cultural traditions. **Alliances** existed between tribes for trade, defense, intermarriage, and the exchange of ideas. Warfare between tribes was a regular part of life, but the conflicts were more like **skirmishes** than major warfare. A war party often attacked a village at night, taking valuable items and capturing women and children as slaves. Men who could not defend a village were killed or run off.

DID YOU KNOW...

Native tribes in the Pacific Northwest held potlatches, or gatherings where a wealthy person gained social status by giving away enormous quantities of possessions. This is very different from modern-day America, where status is measured by how many possessions one keeps for him or herself.

CHAPTER THREE

RISE TO POWER

As a young man, Seattle took part in many battles to protect his people from raiding tribes. He also participated in raids on aggressive tribes to try to stop them from attacking. His clever strategies and bravery as a warrior led his people to trust his strong leadership. But his leadership skills were about to be challenged in new ways as white settlers arrived in the area.

In 1833, the British built a trading post at the south end of Puget Sound. Soon after, small numbers of Americans from New England and the upper Midwest settled nearby and began farming. This was the beginning of white settlement in the area. Over time, as more settlers came, the clash between the two cultures grew.

The first trading post in the Puget Sound area was established by Hudson's Bay Company.

Not only did settlers try to take Native American land when they came to Puget Sound, they also brought disease to the region, which killed many of Seattle's people.

During that time, both England and the United States claimed possession of the area, which was called the Oregon Country. Both governments believed that Native Americans were inferior humans who could not govern themselves. Because the two governments did not respect Native American ways, they tried to force tribes to give up their own traditions and adopt white ways.

★ ★ ★ ★
What might have happened if Chief Seattle had chosen not to cooperate with the white settlers?

Chief Seattle was in a difficult position in deciding how to respond to pressures to change. He understood that the arrival of white settlers in the Puget Sound area eventually would cause the extinction of his people's traditional way of life.

Chief Seattle wanted to protect his people's lives and well-being as much as possible. He also believed that his people would benefit from learning new ways. He saw that the metal tools of the settlers helped them build

Missionaries preach to Native Americans in the woods. These sessions changed Chief Seattle's view on religion.

homes, plow the land, and protect themselves more easily. Chief Seattle decided that he could best help his people by cooperating with and learning from the settlers.

During this time, white **missionaries** spread Christianity among the tribes, believing it was better than Native religions. In the late 1840s, Chief Seattle converted to Catholicism and took the name Noe, after the prophet Noah. His conversion strengthened his relationship with the settlers by making it clear that he meant to cooperate with them. Chief Seattle also started morning and evening prayer services among his people.

DID YOU KNOW...

Chief Seattle married twice. Before her death, his first wife bore a daughter, called Princess Angeline by white settlers. His second wife bore five children, both daughters and sons. Chief Seattle's conversion to Catholicism followed the death of one of his sons.

Princess Angeline

Settlers traveled on the Oregon Trail to reach western North America. One in ten people died along the way, many from diseases caused by poor sanitation.

Over the years, settlers continued to move westward across North America. In 1846, the Oregon Country officially became a U.S. territory. As settlers came to the Puget Sound area in greater numbers, tensions rose between them and Native peoples.

In 1853, the U.S. government separated Washington Territory from Oregon Territory, and the new governor, Isaac Stevens, arrived in the Puget Sound area. His job was to make **treaties** with Native tribes in order to take their land from them and move them to **reservations**. He welcomed the destruction of Native culture and mistakenly believed that they did, too.

Issac Stevens was in charge of treaties with the Native Americans.

Chief Seattle understood that there was no point in fighting the settlers, who had better weapons and greatly outnumbered his people. If he cooperated, his people would be moved to reservation land. If he didn't cooperate, war and killing would result, and his people might not have any place to live at all.

In 1852, Dr. David Maynard named the community of Seattle after his close friend, Chief Seattle.

Chief Seattle maintained friendships with the settlers and encouraged trade, hoping to blend his people's future with the future of the settlers' new community. However, Chief Seattle's dream of a community that blended both cultures did not come to pass. The white people in power, wanting the land for their own, did their best to keep the two cultures separate. As a result, as more settlers came to the Puget Sound area, traditional tribal ways began to disappear.

DID YOU KNOW... The Suquamish people believed that to mention a dead person's name frequently would disturb that person's eternal rest. When white settlers took Chief Seattle's name for their settlement, he taxed them a small amount of money regularly to make up for the unrest his spirit would suffer after death.

CHAPTER FOUR

POINT ELLIOTT TREATY AND ITS AFTERMATH

G overnor Stevens negotiated the Point Elliott Treaty with the Puget Sound tribes. The treaty stated that the tribes had to give up much of their land and move to reservations. The tribes could continue to fish where they always had fished and to hunt and gather on all unclaimed land. They were supposed to be friendly to white settlers and maintain peaceful relations with other tribes except in self-defense.

On Jan. 22, 1855, leaders from more than 20 Puget Sound tribes signed the treaty. Chief Seattle was the first to sign. By agreeing to the terms of the treaty, tribes gave up control of enormous areas of land. Chief Seattle's tribe, the Suquamish, gave up more than 87,000 acres to the United States and only was able to keep about 7,500 acres, which was named the Port Madison Indian Reservation.

TREATY
BETWEEN
THE UNITED STATES
AND THE
DWAMISH, SUQUAMISH, AND OTHER ALLIED AND
SUBORDINATE TRIBES OF INDIANS IN
WASHINGTON TERRITORY.

JANUARY 22, 1855. RATIFIED APRIL 11, 1859.

The U.S. government signed treaties that it did not honor.

Dr. Henry A. Smith

Before signing the treaty, Chief Seattle made a speech about the future of his people. That speech has become very **controversial** because no one knows exactly what he said and many different versions of the speech exist. The speech's accuracy is questioned because participants in the treaty negotiations spoke different languages, so there were many opportunities for translation mistakes. The most widely accepted version was published by Dr. Henry A. Smith in an 1887 newspaper column, more than 30 years after the speech was given. Historians disagree about whether Dr. Smith knew the languages well enough to create an accurate translation.

IN THEIR OWN WORDS

"There was a time when our people covered the whole land...But that time has long since passed away with the greatness of tribes now almost forgotten."

~Chief Seattle, as quoted by Dr. Henry A. Smith

Dr. Smith said that his version of the speech represented the words of Chief Seattle but lacked the grace and seriousness of the original speech. Dr. Smith, who was a writer, also added his own flowery language to Chief Seattle's thoughts. Modern-day Suquamish people consider Dr. Smith's version to be accurate except for the writing style, but much controversy still exists.

Coast Salish basket

Chief Seattle's own tribe, the Suquamish, believe that his peaceful leadership helped his people during a painful time in their history and allowed them to survive to the present day. But not everyone agrees. Some Native Americans believe that Chief Seattle abandoned his people by siding with the settlers. A leader of the Klallam tribe referred to Chief Seattle as "a low type of Indian, a joke among the Natives and worse, a coward and a traitor" for being so cooperative during treaty negotiations and for giving up Native lands to the U.S. government.

Chief Seattle wanted the settlers to respect the nature of Puget Sound.

According to Dr. Smith, Chief Seattle placed one hand on the head of Governor Stevens while giving his speech. He raised the index finger of his other hand, pointing toward the sky.

In his speech, Chief Seattle expressed fear that his people's traditional way of life would end and that they would die out completely. He stated that he wanted his people to live peacefully with the settlers and the new culture they brought to the Puget Sound area. In return, he asked the settlers to respect his people and the places where their ancestors were buried. He also asked them to respect the natural world, as his people did.

Other versions of the speech also have been published. One was written by a professor named Ted Perry in the early 1970s for a movie about ecology. It includes a variation of the phrase "How can one sell the air?" for which Chief Seattle is often given credit. This version was wrongly credited to Chief Seattle by the movie's producers and has been published around the world. Perry's speech, which has inspired people to live in harmony with the environment, has made Chief Seattle famous for words he never spoke.

COUNTERPOINT
Present Day Challenges

Many people believe that giving credit to Chief Seattle for Ted Perry's speech stereotypes Native Americans as valuing nature above everything else. In truth, many tribes today face difficult choices in trying to balance a respect for nature with the need to make money. Some very poor tribes have the opportunity to use their natural resources to help them escape poverty. For example, they must decide whether to allow dumpsites on their land and whether to sell the rights to their timber and minerals. The money brought in may provide jobs, new homes, college scholarships, and a more hopeful future.

After Chief Seattle's speech and the signing of the Point Elliott Treaty, some tribal leaders were unclear about what they had agreed to. As it became clearer that the Native Americans would lose most of their land and would be forced to share reservations with tribes that had different languages and customs, many people became angry.

Leschi, of the Nisqually tribe in the South Puget Sound, was one of the leaders in the uprising against white settlers. He was later captured and hanged.

From 1855 to 1858, Native Americans tried to drive out the white settlers in an uprising called the Yakima War. Many tribes in western Washington and Oregon participated in the uprising, but Chief Seattle kept the Suquamish out of it.

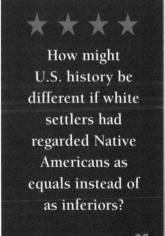

★ ★ ★ ★

How might U.S. history be different if white settlers had regarded Native Americans as equals instead of as inferiors?

Native Americans came to Seattle by steamer to collect land payments from the government.

The warring tribes were defeated because they were poorly organized and had no experience fighting a long battle. Tribal leaders were driven into the Cascade Mountains, where they were killed or captured. After the war, it became clear that the tribes had no choice but to live peacefully on reservations.

Over time, Puget Sound tribes became more and more **impoverished**, partly because it took four years for the U.S. government to formally approve the treaty. During that time, tribes lost most of their land but did not receive promised blankets, supplies, or money to help them move to reservations. It was a time of great hardship, and many people starved to death.

IN THEIR OWN WORDS

"I fear that we are forgotten or that we are to be cheated out of our land." *~Chief Seattle, more than three years after the Port Elliott Treaty was signed*

When Chief Seattle's people began reservation life, the U.S. government tried to put an end to Suquamish traditions. People no longer had access to many of their fishing, hunting, and

Chief Seattle's grave is located in a Native American cemetery next to St. Peter's Church on the Port Madison Indian Reservation.

gathering grounds. Ceremonies and religious practices were outlawed. Children could no longer learn tribal languages. Old Man House, the winter house of Chief Seattle and his people, was burned.

Chief Seattle died on the Port Madison Indian Reservation in early June, 1866, at the age of 81. He was buried at St. Peter's Church cemetery in the town of Suquamish.

Chief Seattle's gravestone

DID YOU KNOW... Although the city of Seattle was named after him, Chief Seattle's death was not reported there and was not publicized until Dr. Smith's 1887 newspaper column was printed. The year before his death, it became illegal for Native Americans to own permanent houses within city limits.

CHAPTER FIVE

CHIEF SEATTLE'S PEOPLE TODAY

The Suquamish and several other tribes continue to live on the Port Madison Indian Reservation. The reservation, which lies across Puget Sound from the city of Seattle, is an independent nation with its own laws and government.

Tribal leaders are still working to force the U.S. government to honor the terms of the Point Elliott Treaty regarding fishing and hunting rights. Conservation efforts are bringing back the sea otter, which was close to extinction. Salmon and timber, which also were **depleted**, are coming back. The area is recovering, but much work still needs to be done.

The story of Chief Seattle's life marks the entrance to his grave site.

The Suquamish are working to preserve their native language. In the year 2000, fewer than 60 native speakers of the language existed. Suquamish children are now learning the language in school.

Present-day Native Americans dance during Chief Seattle Days in Suquamish, Washington.

Each summer, the Suquamish tribe holds an event called Chief Seattle Days, a celebration of Suquamish culture held in honor of Chief Seattle. In 1983, the tribe established the Suquamish Museum to "preserve, protect, and exhibit tribal culture, history, and artifacts." People from all over the world visit the museum to learn about Native cultures in the Pacific Northwest. Tribal leaders are working hard to build a strong future for their people.

IN THEIR OWN WORDS

"Knowing some of the early settlers as well as he did, the fact that the small village bearing his name survived and flourished would not surprise him. That his people have survived the challenges of this century would please him."

~from the 1985 Suquamish publication The Eyes of Chief Seattle

CONCLUSION

Chief Seattle led his people through the most difficult time in their history. During his lifetime, as outsiders **assaulted** his culture, the responsibility rested on his shoulders to guide his people wisely through the challenges.

We'll never know the complete truth about Chief Seattle or why he decided to cooperate so fully with white settlers and the U.S. government. We do know that leaders throughout history often have been faced with impossibly difficult choices. Chief Seattle did his best to make wise decisions on behalf of his people. Their survival and pride in their culture are evidence of his success.

A life-size copper statue of Chief Seattle was unveiled in the city of Seattle on November 13, 1912.